I die daily

*compiled from
teaching transcripts*

by
Pastor Star R. Scott

Copyright © 2012 by Pastor Star R. Scott.

All rights reserved. No portion of this book may be reproduced, stored in a retrieval system or transmitted in any form or by any means - electronic, mechanical, photocopying, recording, or any other - without the written permission of the copyright owner.
Published in Sterling, Virginia. Published by Star Publishing.

Calvary Temple
50214 Triple Seven Road
Sterling, VA 20165
(703) 430-7307
www.calvarytempleva.org

All Scripture quotations are from the King James Version of the Bible (KJV).

ISBN-13: 978-1-938520-05-1

Other Books by Pastor Star R. Scott

Adam's Rib
Headship, Helpmeet & Lovers

The Goodness of Grace

Worldly Wagons or Sanctified Shoulders

Holiness
Jesus' Imminent Return

Holiness
The Holy Pastor

Holiness
We Shall Be Like Him
Volumes 1-4

Prevailing in Prayer

Walking in the Spirit
Volumes 1-4

Feed My Sheep
Principles of Godly Leadership

Divine Guidance

Table of Contents

Publisher's Note vii
The Cross: Defined...1
Doctrine vs. Application..3
Cross, Test, Persecution, or Chastisement 5
Choose the Cross...8
Embrace the Cross...10
The Cost of the Cross 12
Don't Try, Just Die..14
Stop and Pray..16
Death to Self: A Habit You Can Live With 18
Dead People Don't Suffer..20
You Get What You Want..22
Empty Yourself..24
Who Will You Deny?...26
Expressions of Self 28
What is Love?..30
Remove the Beam and Check the Speck 33
Christ's Personal Cross 36
Do What You Are Told..39
Where's Your Mark?..41
Worthy To Be Called Disciple 43
Not A Partnership 45

Created For His Glory 47
God Can Use Dead Men 50
Resignation to God's Will 52
Will You Follow? 54
The Cross is Obedience 56
Love Him More 58
The World is Crucified
to Me 60
Persecution 62
Weights, Sins, and Distractions 64
Distractions 66

Publisher's Note

The work you hold in your hands is a compilation of sermon transcripts that Pastor Star Scott has delivered to his Sterling, Virginia congregation during 40 years of ministry there. While using segments of transcriptions is certainly not the most common format for a published work, the possibility of doing so was approached with care and deliberation.

In recent years, with the republication of older Christian literature, some publishers have taken considerable license in editing the writing of great authors who have since gone home to be with the Lord. This seems to have been done in the interest of making the writings more palatable for today's Christian reader. Because of our interest in maintaining the integrity of the doctrine and even retaining the anointing that was on these messages as they were originally delivered, we have decided to present them here in transcribed form.

Perhaps the most direct admonition to take this approach came from one of the great pioneers of the Pentecostal movement in the twentieth century, Willard Cantelon. Cantelon, who was truly an eloquent man, and mighty in the scriptures, considered Pastor Scott to be his spiritual pastor and dear friend. In a personal letter to Scott, Cantelon encouraged him: "I am sure that recording your sermons on tape is one of the 'wisest' things you do. And knowing that these messages can be transcribed in writing and find their way to the different 'levels' of readers in the days ahead is a long-range vision that is most real." In another letter, Cantelon continued by saying, "There is something special about what is delivered 'live' and printed the way it is given." We certainly agree with Brother Cantelon's perspective on these matters and therefore present these timely yet timeless teachings in such a format.

As you prepare for the soon return of our Lord and seek to strengthen your relationship with Father, we pray that you will be helped, challenged, and enriched by these teachings.

CHAPTER ONE

The Cross: Defined

When I say, "taking up our cross," many of us confuse that with Paul's thorn in the flesh. "Well, that's just my cross that I have to bear." No, **the cross is, for every one of us, identical—it is death to self.** The cross is dying to self-ness, personal ambition, self-righteousness, and independence. In every way and in every day, we are called to embrace that cross. We need to prepare our hearts. We need to realize that in the midst of adversity—in the midst of afflictions and temptations and persecutions—there is the necessity of embracing the cross.

The cross is different than trials, afflictions, persecutions, and temptations. Those are things that are put upon us. The cross, however, is pursued. The cross is a choice, and Jesus made that very clear when he said, "If any man will come after me..." (Matthew 16:24, Luke 9:23) The difference is volition, which is the choice of personal death on a daily basis. **It is important for us to see that the cross, however, is often ignored until the outward pressures of afflictions, persecutions, and trials are thrust upon us. There is nothing in the natural man that seeks the cross.**

I like a statement that Tozer made in one of his books. He said, "The problem with Christianity today is that the cross has become a token of life instead of the reality of death." He further stated, "Today, Christians wear the cross; and in the early church, the cross wore the Christian." That is quite a statement if you meditate upon that a little bit. We are going to be unable to count it joy when all of the adversities come our way without having embraced the cross. We are going to, like everybody else, begin to have self-pity and fears.

When I say "fear," I am talking about anxiety or worry. The Bible says, "*Be* [anxious] *for nothing; but in every thing* [through] *prayer and supplication with thanksgiving...*" (Philippians 4:6). Are you thankful for the circumstances that you are in? Have you put away worry, anxiety, and all of these things that are driving us to self-preservation; or are we allowing these things to be embraced? We must allow them to bring us—instead of to self-preservation—to self-crucifixion, which will enable us to die to these things. A dead man does not worry. And a dead man does not fear. A dead man has no reputation and does not care what anybody thinks about him. The seeking of the praises of men, rather than that of God, is the pressure of the hour.

CHAPTER TWO

Doctrine vs. Application

Do not be content with good doctrine, good habits, and a good foundation. I did not say to not recognize the value of the foundation of the apostles, prophets, and Jesus himself—the chief cornerstone; however, the apostle said, "Take heed how you build thereon." Another way to say that is, "take care to actually apply doctrine to your life."

Having both good doctrine and the understanding of how it works is tremendous. Knowing the Word of God is great, but what we are talking about is death to self. Do you know that Matthew 18 cannot work if one of those two people is alive? Did you know that the Ephesians passages on marriage cannot work if one of those people is still alive? You are unable to love your wife as your own body if you are alive. A wife cannot submit to her husband as unto the Lord if she is still alive. None of it works. All of the conflicts that you find yourself in are because of self--self-will and self-righteousness—this ego and selfness that seems to think that we know better.

In trying to make the cross practical, some very obvious words come to mind. Words that you love to hear, such as "humility" and "love." Do you ever have a tendency to think of yourself more highly than you ought to think? You may be able to quote 1 Corinthians 13, but do you live it? What do you do under pressure or when you don't get your way? How about when you're not well spoken of? What do you habitually do when there's an opportunity to forego what you want to do and prefer others? Where is the fruit of servant hood? How likely are you to gird that towel and wash others' feet when you are not being seen, or there is nothing for you to get out of it? This is not just theoretical or theological—we must carry this very practical approach to the cross.

CHAPTER THREE

Cross, Test, Persecution, or Chastisement

I want to begin to draw some distinctions between the cross, tests, persecutions, and chastisement. Many of us call a cross (or persecution or trial) what is, in fact, chastisement. Making a distinction between these four instances can be difficult.

The first thing that I like to look at whenever I begin to see that there is adversity or a loss of peace or an unclear course before me is to step back and ask myself the question: "Father, what place am I in that's bringing this lack of peace in my life? Am I now in unbelief? Am I at a place where I'm depleted spiritually, and because of that, I've really lost that capacity in the midst of adversity to trust and rely and have assurance (that's what faith is) in Your promises? Am I in the midst of a test, right now, of my faith, and it seems that I'm coming up short here and lacking?"

If that's the case, there's an easy solution to that. Faith comes by hearing, and hearing by the Word of God. I need to have an audience with God. I need to do whatever it takes to get into the presence of God. Beloved, when you find these things upon yourself, you need to pray and ask God what's going on. If you lack wisdom, if you lack understanding of this dilemma that you find yourself in, ask God, who gives to all men liberally and upbraideth not

Cross. Now when I use the term "cross," remember that it always

I Die Daily

has to do with conflict of wills. The cross is subordinating your will to the will of God. The cross isn't hardship; it's not adversity. The cross is not a sickness or persecution that you're bearing. The cross is not that you have to deal with unsaved spouses or children. The cross is dying to self: self-indulgence, independent living, independent thinking, exalting your thoughts and your methods above the wisdom of God. The cross is going to enable you to respond properly to all of these other experiences that are either consequences to your righteousness or chastisement for your carnality.

Test. When God brought the children of Israel into the wilderness, it was a test to prove what was in their hearts. Sometimes that comes through adversity and afflictions and persecution, and sometimes a test comes in a time of lack. There are also times when God will remove from you His manifest presence to see if you'll stand in faith? "I don't feel You. I don't hear You. I don't even know, right now, if I believe in You, but where can I go? You alone have the words of eternal life. So I stand." Then that manifest presence comes, and you know in whom you have believed. Have you ever been there?

Persecution. Now, what do you do when you find yourself in a place where there is persecution in your life? The parable of the sower makes it very clear that when that Word comes and it begins to produce life and faith, there is going to be opposition, and many will be offended at the persecution; but thank God, you are not going to flee under persecution. For in all of these things—Romans 8—you are more than a conqueror. If anything, it creates a greater resolve and a boasting and an expectation of the deliverance of God.

Chastisement. And then there's the chastening of the Lord, and as you try to discern in the wisdom of God, ask, "What is it that's coming upon me, right now?" If it's the chastening of the Lord, then you don't need to pray. There's a time to pray. There's a time of fasting. But right now, you just need to submit, you need to rest, and you need to repent. And just like the judgment of God on Israel following their battle at Ai, you need to get sin out of the camp. You need to determine, "What is it, Lord, that's been an offense to You? What is it that needs to be driven from my life? What are the consequences going to be?"

We've all experienced that in our lives, but you can rest in this comfort: the Lord chastens those that He loves. If you'll endure even to death, you'll receive the crown of life. The chastening that is grievous for the moment—if you don't faint, if you endure—will work in you the peaceable fruit of righteousness.

CHAPTER FOUR

Choose the Cross

We're not worthy to be called His disciples if we're not willing to forsake all and follow Him. And if we don't love Him more than fathers and mothers and brothers and sisters and children and houses and lands and, yes, even our own lives, we're not worthy of Him—think of the magnitude of that statement!

Jesus says to take up our cross daily and follow Him, and we've seen that the cross isn't trials, tribulations, adversities or hard times. The cross that we're encouraged—no—*commanded* to take up is the cross that finally presents and reckons self as dead—the cross of the crucifixion of ego, this self that is in great conflict with God.

However, we have the right to choose the indwelling presence of God. We have the ability to choose to walk in the spirit, and if we walk in the spirit, we will not fulfill the lust of the flesh. The mandate has been given to us—I've set before you this day life and death, therefore choose life (Deuteronomy 30:19). Praise God! So we see that it's a choice that is set before us on a daily basis. It's a choice to either take up that cross and reckon ourselves dead indeed unto sin and alive unto Christ, or to prefer ourselves.

When Paul says, "*...in me, that is, in my flesh*"—he's not talking about the members of this carnal body. He's saying that in the soul-dominated life—dwells no good thing. There are natural appetites in all of us, but they are administrated by the soul's (our emotions, intellect, and will) choices.

So then how do we better discipline the aspects of our lives that we still dictate? How do we discipline our volitions and our choices? How do we subordinate it to the will of God—to the mind of Christ? The answer, of course, is to choose that daily cross. And our spirit is willing, but the flesh is weak. But remember, we can't judge ourselves by our intentions. We might say, "Well, I really have a desire. I want to change. I want to be like Jesus. I want to serve God. I want to prefer the Lord over myself." But we can't accept or believe that if we habitually prefer self over God. Because the Scripture set forth some principles that are irrevocable, and that is when you seek God with all of your heart, you will…? find Him (Jeremiah 29:13). And He will work in you to will and to do of His good pleasure (Philippians 2:13).

So, then, we have to examine our lives and say, "Well, then, you know, I guess I'm not seeking Him with all of my heart." Have you been able to come to that conclusion? Have you discovered the weak link in this whole process is you?

CHAPTER FIVE

Embrace the Cross

Embracing the cross is about giving all for God. Luke 14:26 emphasizes giving up your own life. When you hate all of those things that can become disproportionate in your life – that is when you are embracing the cross. I want to tell you something. You love yourself more than anybody else. "Oh, I love my children more." No, you do not. Don't argue with the Word of God. Every child of Adam and Eve is a self-lover. Jesus says it right there in Luke 14:26 when he talks about "your own life also." He speaks of the vileness of self-love (however that self-love evidences itself in our lives). Many of us have trouble with our own depravity and coming to grips with it, but **until you can realize you love yourself more than anybody else, you are never going to be free.** You start there. You start with the death of self, the death of ego - that part of man that is absolutely in every way representing the natural man's father, the devil who said in Isaiah 14, *"I will ascend above the heights of the clouds; I will be like the most High."*

The embracing of the cross is removing self from the throne. When there is a conflict with the will of God and self, choose God. When there is a conflict between your emotions and the promises of God, choose the promises of God. It's not always easy. It's not always smooth. There are times when you can hear the voice of God and choose it almost as easily as breathing; it's second nature. At other times, it's not that way. You may be battling emotions or all kinds of different internal conflicts, but you must choose the cross. Choose to believe God's Word is true. Choose to believe the wisdom and the goodness of your God. Choose to push down and refuse to entertain the voice of self, and choose to seek the voice of God. Get quiet enough to hear again that voice that says, "This is the way; walk in it."

It is a war. It's daily. It's hourly. Dear God, it's by the minute at times, when every emotion and everything that would exalt itself against the goodness and the promises of God have got to be torn down. You look at the devil and you look into self, and you say, "You're a liar. God is true. His Word is true."

CHAPTER SIX

The Cost of the Cross

A young man once asked Jesus, "What must I do to be saved?" So Jesus put out a few of the standards of the law set forth by the Ten Commandments. Every challenge that Jesus gave him was from the second half of the Commandments, which address relating to men—both socially and morally. And the young man replied, *"All these have I kept from my youth up."* Then Jesus took the whole first half and summarized it in one statement, "[OK then] *sell all that thou hast, and distribute unto the poor... and come, follow me"* (Luke 18:18-23). The man dropped his head and walked away sorrowfully, because he was very rich. Yeah, let's use another word. He was very selfish. He was lord of his own life. He had treasures that were not the Pearl of Great Price. He had ambitions that exceeded servanthood. He preferred himself over Jesus and others. See it for what it is. He created gods of *his* ambition, *his* will, *his* ease, and broke the first and great commandment: *"And thou shalt love the Lord thy God with all thine heart..."* (Deuteronomy 6:5). If you save your life, you will lose it. What does it profit you to have your own way, to fulfill all of your dreams, your goals, your ideologies and lose your own soul? What would you give in exchange for it? What salary? What fame? What fortune would you give in exchange for your soul?

Some of the young people I talk to say, "Yeah, I'm just afraid if I yield everything to God, He's going to ask me to do something I don't want." If you keep part of your life, you're going to lose it all. How about it, college kids? You say things like, "Whatever we do for the Lord, we're to do it with all of our might." Are you really doing that for the Lord? "Amen!" What if He tells you to quit? What if you're in the last half of the last semester, and He says, "I've got something for you to do, come and follow Me. I'm sending you to Africa"? Sadly, most would reply, "Oh, thank you. Only one more month and my finals, and I'm there, man!" He didn't say anything about that. Can I ask you a question, Mom, Dad? What's your counsel going to be? Some of us are not even about the credits, we're about the dollars. "Do you know what that will cost?" Yeah, I'll tell you what this thing costs. It costs everything!

Philippians 3:14 says, "I press toward the mark." In the Greek that means, "I am fully emptied out. I'm stretched forth with all that's within me. There's not an ounce of strength left, there's nothing more that I can do, that I might win '...*the prize of the high calling of God.*'" Would you give yourself that evaluation? And if not, can you find a Scripture that makes that acceptable? Were Abraham, Elijah, and Paul the exceptions? Or were they men with like passions? There is a great cloud of witnesses standing out there saying, "What's up with you guys?" You see, beloved, this is normative Christianity. Jesus is coming back, and His Bride is making herself ready. Are you?

Don't Try, Just Die

Matthew 16:24, *"Then said Jesus unto his disciples, If any man will come after me, let him deny himself, and take up his cross, and follow me."* This message of the cross, this message of the Gospel is not a cheap message; it cost the holy blood of God. But very frankly, my heart is grieved at the cheapness that people have put upon that blood. People have tried to dilute and minimize the cost of the cross because of the idols that they have raised in their own hearts. They want a crossless Christianity, but there is no such thing. They come into the house of God and just kick around and say, "What do you want from me? I said that I am seeking the Lord. I'm saying the right words. Get off my back. What more do you want from me?!" Death! I'm asking you to die.

As a representative of Jesus, as one who proclaims the Gospel of Jesus Christ, what I'm asking of you is this: **If you're going to call yourself a Christian, die! If you're going to call yourself a Christian, then strive to enter in.** If you're going to call yourself a Christian, then identify with the Apostle Paul and proclaim that whatever used to be your treasure, you now call dung that you might win Christ. That sacrifice of everything is what I'm asking of you—not your crumbs. This is not a social club. This is not Thanksgiving family gathering. We're not here for your entertainment. This is the holy tabernacle of God Almighty. And we come together as the Church, the temple of God, for one purpose: to glorify God. The zeal of His house should eat us up. The jealousy for the glory of God.

How *dare* we let people carry their trash through the Temple of God! Where are the whips to come and drive them out of our midst? But instead it's, "No. Oh poor little thing. Wipe their nose. They're trying their hardest." Die! Don't try, just die! "Well, they said they were really wanting to seek the Lord and that they have made a confession and have accepted Jesus as Lord." I don't believe it! Because the Bible that I read says, "We become a new creation"—not whitewashed, not people that resolve to do better—a new creation. *"...old things are passed away; behold, all things are become new."* (2 Corinthians 5:17). Isn't that what happened to you when you got saved? So then, why are you trying to make excuses for yourself and those closest to you? There's no new Gospel. The path isn't broader. There are no family exemptions. There is *no* other way to enter into this kingdom. Just die!

CHAPTER EIGHT

Stop and Pray

Do you think you know the will of God? Have you already determined what will bring the most glory to God? Peter thought he knew. Jesus started to tell his disciples in Matthew 16:22, "*how that he must go unto Jerusalem, and suffer many things of the elders and chief priests and scribes, and be killed, and be raised again the third day.*" And Peter rebukes Jesus in verse 23, saying, "*Be it far from thee, Lord: this shall not be unto thee.*" Peter was really saying, "Not so, Lord! I already have it figured out. Here's how You're going to manifest Your will. You're going to show Your power in this way. You're going to be exalted. You're going to deliver Israel from Rome, and I believe I'll probably be sitting at Your right hand." And how did Jesus respond to that attitude? "Get behind me, Satan." What Jesus was saying here was, "You're seeking the things of men and not of God."

Do you think you've ever made decisions or determinations that would have caused that kind of a response from the Master? How many times have you second-guessed Him? **How many times have you known better what would glorify God and didn't even *ask* how He would have you administrate His Word or His will?**

Jesus said, in John 8:29, "*I do always those things that please* [My Father]." Don't you want that to be your testimony? When that begins

Stop and Pray

to be the real cry of your heart, a couple of things will happen: You will begin to pause before making decisions because your life has become a vessel for the glory of God, and you will actually *ask* Him before doing something. You will pray in the midst of whatever it is you're doing, because you're to do everything as unto the Lord and with all of your might.

CHAPTER NINE

Death to Self: A Habit You Can Live With

Do any of you have the habit of going to the gym? Do you have the habit of a life of recreation or ease? Do you have the habit of watching whatever TV program you like? Do you have the habit of, when you get home, sitting in your recliner or going out to the garage to tinker? We all have habits, and we do them in repetition. It's just second nature to us.

Can I ask you a question? Is it second nature to you to deny yourself? Is it a habit? Is righteousness a habit? Is obedience a habit? Can you deny yourself without even thinking about it? Can you say, "Get out of here, self. You need to subordinate!" Until you can get to that place, then, I would question the dominance of the life of Christ in your life. I would say that you're probably still in danger.

"Well, you know, Pastor, I believe what I choose habitually is the kingdom of God, and the will of God, and the Word of God." Praise God, we all know what habits do then, don't we? They demand and dictate. Through repetition, desire comes. This denial, the habitual denial of self, is similar to when the Scripture speaks to us and says, "... *by reason of use have* [your] *senses exercised to discern both good and evil*" (Hebrews 5:14). By constant, persistent, habitual submission to the will and wisdom of God, you become sensitized to know what's not

Death to Self: A Habit You Can Live With

of God. Your choices must be habitually exercised to judge properly between good and evil. Good is anything that God is telling you to do. Evil is anything that self is telling you to do that would conflict with the heart of God, the purposes of God.

How do you know when you've embraced the cross? Who do you habitually choose when there's a conflict of your desires—what society and psychology and the fruit from the Garden of Eden say are your rights and your responsibilities—and you're offered the cross? *"Come and follow me."* I guarantee you one thing. Your flesh will rise up in you and say, "This is too much. This doesn't sound like it's necessary. I think…" We judge the cross foolish and want to retain a portion of our lives, a right, a vote, a say, and we are not our own.

So the challenge of that death; how does this take place? What causes it? God allows us to experience it in many ways, but it's just a clash of selfishness, selfness, against the Lordship of Jesus Christ. When that clash takes place, how would you truthfully analyze yourself? What do you choose habitually?

CHAPTER TEN

Dead People Don't Suffer

Do you feel like you're suffering? Are you in turmoil? Then you're not dead to self. **Until you die, you will never be able to make the right decision. When you're dead, you'll be able to make it according to the will of God without emotion, without fear, without prejudice and in absolute tranquility that even if you make the wrong decision, He sets your paths right.** When you're dead you do not suffer. If you were completely dead to your old nature, you would no longer feel many of the things that now bother you.

Are you bothered that people have misunderstood you? Maybe they've said bad things about you? They don't appreciate you? What's bothering you? How touchy are you? Does it bother you that nobody else sees you the way you see yourself? You're not dead. You should only be concerned with one thing: How does Jesus see you? How does the Word of God reflect your image as the image of Christ? God prepares a cross for you that must be embraced without thought of self-preservation.

The pain of resisting the cross is harder to live with than the cross itself. Why don't you give up? Oh dear God, I can't tell you the times in my prayer closet over these last years, when I've just laid there before

God - broken and crying, and He says, "Why don't you give up?" And do you know what? Over these last years I've given up a lot of times. I've died, and then here I am again! **Does anybody else keep having the wrong resurrection?**

That's why you need brothers and sisters in Christ. Yet somebody comes to try to hold you down, and you want to fight them all the way and say things like, "Hey, you're not showing love! Who do you think you are? Yeah, well what about your sins?" The dude is just trying to hold you in the grave. Thank him, praise God. What about saying, "Thank you, man. I appreciate it. Dear God, you know that guy you're talking about - my flesh? I hate him, man. Let's get together and whip the tar out of him." Die. Resisting the cross is harder than embracing the cross; and ultimately if you continue to resist, there will be no more grace and no more compulsion because what you treasure and what you do habitually is who you are, and the cross has become a doctrine to you and not a treasure.

CHAPTER ELEVEN

You Get What You Want

I've found that when I really want ice cream, I get it. Nothing stands in my way. "Neither rain, nor snow, nor sleet, nor hail." Do you normally get what you want? Well, you might not have gotten it yet, but you're still after it. Aren't you?

I think it's interesting when people say things like, "Well, I really want to do what's right. I really want to give all that I have to the Lord." Some people leave themselves a little bit of wiggle room or at least in trying to not be presumptuous, say, "I'm willing to be willing." But those comments are contrary to the Word of God. If you are going to believe those statements, then you have to disbelieve Jesus, who said that those who hunger and thirst after righteousness - what's the next word? - "shall" be filled (Matthew 5:6). You see, you don't want it. You would like to have it if it didn't cost you too much. You would like to have it if you could retain one percent of your life to yourself. But you can have none.

That is the daily battle, and that is the decision that many people truly have never made. Are you aware of what you are holding back from God? Or do you just know that you haven't yielded everything and that you need help in identifying? Well, first of all, you haven't wanted to know it very badly, because the revelation is only as far as the petitioning of God to show you. James 1:5 makes it very clear, *"If any of you lack wisdom, let him ask of God, that giveth to all men liberally and upbraideth not."* You have not because you ask not. There is no greater degree of pride than to say, "I'm seeking with all of my heart and for some reason I'm different, and it won't happen for me." God is no respecter of persons.

Deuteronomy 4:29 says, *"But if from thence thou shalt seek the* LORD *thy God, thou shalt find him, if thou seek him with all thy heart and with all thy soul."* Yet you give up on prayer, and you give up on studying the Word. You give up on fasting, and serving others, and denying yourself. And it's because you have not put proper value on that Pearl of Great Price.

Don't say, "I'm trying." Trying what? Trying to find another route? Another way? There is only one way: it's a way of death. It's a straight and narrow way. It's not a way of 99 percent. It's the way of the cross, and you're just going to have to die.

CHAPTER TWELVE

Empty Yourself

Although our actions are the byproduct of choosing the lordship of Jesus and the will of God, the cross itself does not have a lot to do with works or performances, but rather the motive behind them. What I'm saying is this: too often people can begin to do good things that are only motivated by self will. "I am going to cut this out of my life. I'm going to get rid of all of these things." This, of course, is not a license for those of you who want to hold on to all of your earthly stuff. Don't start rejoicing. I'm not done yet, but the fact of the matter is that God does want to bless you. You have a good Father from whom every good and perfect gift comes. So rejoice in His goodness. It is not noble to push away the blessings that God wants to bestow upon you at a given time. That is asceticism, and it only makes you think you have somehow become nobler in the eyes of others. God is not looking for works. He's looking for obedience. Sometimes God wants you to take His blessings. Sometimes you are to offer up the blessings of your own volition. Sometimes you have to be willing to turn loose of what He's taking from you.

Ask yourself this question: have I truly been emptied of self? **The emptying of self is what the cross is all about. The cross is the daily pursuit of discovering and knowing the heart and will of God. It is**

purposing to destroy everything within us that would oppose God's will either by perversion or opposition. By praying for the will of God, you are making a declaration that you will resign yourself to His wisdom, His will, and His way and not your own. Empty yourself and embrace the cross. That may seem radical to your flesh and the world, but it is normative to the Kingdom of God, the true Church, and Biblical Christianity.

CHAPTER THIRTEEN

Who Will You Deny?

Matthew 10:33 makes it very clear that if you deny Jesus before men, He will deny you before the Father. **To prefer self is to deny Jesus. And to deny self is to prefer Jesus.** To make decisions without consideration of His Lordship is to deny Him. How many decisions did you make today without considering His Lordship? Many of the things that you trivialize are just indicators of how self-sufficient and independent and unaware of the presence of God you really are on a daily basis.

When you pray in the morning, are you asking Father, "What would you have me to do today?" Or do you say, "Why should I bother? I know what I'm going to do. I have to go to work." Really? What if the Master addresses you just like he did Levi, and says, "You're leaving work today. Come and follow Me"? Are you even in a place right now where you could hear that voice?

I'm sure you are a busy person. You say, "I've got stuff to do, places to go and people to see." If you don't have time in the day to think about Jesus, then you're too busy. If you don't have enough time in the day to pause and say, "Lord, what would you have me to do?" then you're too busy! Is your schedule so rigid that you are totally unaware of the voice of the Holy Spirit? I would venture to guess that God is penciled into your schedule somewhere. And you say with pride, "Look! I made room for God today." But God doesn't want to fill just one slot in your Day-Timer.

The word *deny*, as it's used in the Greek, is a very strong word, and it means to absolutely fail to recognize, to associate with, or to give any credibility to the confidence that we have. Taking up the cross and denying self, beloved, is to be crucified with Christ. And so you start quoting Galatians 2:20, "*I am crucified with Christ nevertheless, I live; yet not I, but Christ that liveth in me...*" But having the proper doctrine and being able to quote the Scriptures isn't enough. The question that I want to ask is this: Are you walking the walk? Are you daily embracing this cross? Are you denying yourself?

CHAPTER FOURTEEN

Expressions of Self

In every conflict of will and preference, do you prefer the presence of God, the kingdom of God, the body of Christ, and the highest calling of all—to be least, to be the servant? After making that decision, and knowing that you have embraced the cross, don't you just wish that it would carry on forever like that? How many of you, the very next hour, the very next day or sometime that week, get humbled again by the preference of self, the rising up of the old man? So how do you live out that victory, which Jesus has won for you? First, you must realize that you are a child of Adam, born in total depravity, and that sin is ever present in your members. If you can come to grips with that, then all you have to do is constantly reckon as dead the old man, the flesh. It must be a reckoning, an acknowledgement that causes you to be ever on guard against that voice of the self man, the Adamic nature rising up.

The more you embrace the cross of Jesus Christ, the less bold you will be to speak your opinions all the time. You will not demand conformity of all those around you to perceive as you perceive—as it relates to matters of conscience. You will not overestimate your own worth by demanding others to love you in a certain way - the selfishness that says, "It's not love if you don't love me this way, the way I want to be loved, the way I perceive love to be." Instead, God will be at work within you to will and to do of His good pleasure, as it says in Philippians 2:13. And the same Holy Spirit that is speaking to you, demanding your death, is demanding it also of those around you. And, guess what? They will not necessarily die in the way you think they should die. One of the greatest expressions of self and pride is demanding that others die like you do. Beloved, check your own hearts. Don't say, "Well, if I'm going to be miserable, he's going to be miserable." This death to self isn't "being miserable." It's being free! If you are miserable, you still have other idols.

CHAPTER FIFTEEN

What is Love?

If it's hard for you to die to self to prefer God, then how hard is it to die to self to prefer others? As you are dying, don't make it just an individual event. We are to see a corporate death taking place here, but it will happen one life at a time. *"For the eyes of the LORD [search] to and fro throughout the whole earth, [He is looking for somebody in which] to show Himself strong in behalf of them whose heart is perfect toward Him"* (2 Chronicles 16:9). Most of us, from the natural, think, "Praise God! Somebody who is moving as Elijah did—calling fire down and raising the dead!" He is looking for somebody who will be servant of all. There is no higher calling.

As the disciples reasoned among themselves who should be the greatest, the Lord brought them some instruction and some reproof; He made it very clear to them the necessity of taking on that childlike spirit and humbling themselves, because the greatest among us will surely be the servant of all (Mark 9:33-37).

Until you are able to really embrace the cross and experience death to self, the spiritual relationships you have been commanded to form will become a feigned love filled with hypocrisy and pretense. There is to be commonness and unity between you and your brothers in the Lord, but it is to be based upon the mutual pursuit of Christ-likeness.

What is Love?

It is not commonness and unity based upon a natural (*phileo* or *storge*) love but true godly (*agape*) love. **Love is helping that individual to become more like Jesus today than they were yesterday.** Don't give or accept anything else as love.

That kind of godly love will express itself in many ways. It will express itself in kindness, gentleness, and longsuffering. It will lift up hands that are hanging down, and it will strengthen the feeble knees. But it will also be the agent of chastisement, because the Lord chastens those whom He loves. To be able to love effectively, you need to be able to first die to self-to take the beam out of our own eye—so you can see clearly to help your brothers. Your love is still a selfish love if all you are doing is trying to get yourself ready for Jesus. The more pure you become, then the more free and capable you are of helping them become more like Jesus, so that He would be glorified by much fruit; praise God!

As you die to self, it will produce true Biblical love, which will allow Father to reveal and glorify the person of Jesus to a lost and dying world, because the Scripture makes it very clear that they are going to look at you. And what they need to conclude is this: "Behold how they love one another" (John 13:35). It has nothing to do with the fact that you hang out, bake someone a pie, or drive someone to the doctor's office. The heathen do that! The Mormons do that! See, that's the problem; people think they are loving, but all they are doing is worshipping creatures. That is not love; love is not worshipping a creature and defying the holiness of God. That's the love of self; that's the love of the idol. See, you are to love everybody; but you are to be jealous for the holiness of God, for the truth of God. Be ever ready to give the mercy of God and to show the grace of God, but according to biblical precedent. You are living to make that person eternally better, spiritually better. Yes, the natural aspects are involved also. If you have the wherewithal, you cannot say you love God, whom you have not seen, when you won't love and meet the needs of your brothers, who you have seen. But your *koinonia*—your fellowship— should be around the kingdom of God, the eternal perspective.

Instead of predetermining which of your best friends you are going to hang out with, why don't you ask "Lord, who would *You* have me spend time with?" Moving out of your comfort zone in that way will break the familiarity of the schedule which so often blocks the voice of God. As you begin to die to self, you'll hear the voice of God telling you to pray for them and see them healed, to speak a word of wisdom that removes confusion and doubt from their lives. All because the Holy Spirit was able to orchestrate the Body of Christ, and not your habits or schedules.

What value do you put on achieving the high status of Servant of All? How much of that is your own ambition? Some of us think we would really like to teach a class, or preach, or sing, or whatever; there is nothing wrong with any of that, but what's your motive? Is your motive to put yourself forth, or is your motive to serve where God has placed you and boast in the gifts that God has given you? What I mean by boast is not going around saying, "Look how great this gift is!" I'm talking about being thankful for what God has given you to do; I'm talking about being thankful for the privilege of serving where you serve, even as a doorkeeper in the house of the Lord, to be the servant of all.

CHAPTER SIXTEEN

Remove the Beam and Check the Speck

Another aspect of embracing the cross and death to self is the requirement to love your neighbor as yourself. Biblical love includes bringing reproof, rebuke, doctrine, and instruction into righteousness—as Paul says in the book of Timothy—that the man of God might be perfect and thoroughly furnished unto every good work. As you are obligated to get into the lives of your brothers and sisters in Christ, it's to provoke them to love and to good works, to be that iron that sharpens iron. **Sharpening your brother will never work effectively if you aren't moving in a spirit of humility and love.** You must be driven both by compassion and also by a love and a zeal for the glory of God. You should want to make those around you better that God might be more glorified. Help build up vessels that could contain the glory of God.

Jesus said, in Matthew 7:5, "*First cast out the beam out of thine own eye; and then shalt thou see clearly to cast out the mote out of thy brother's eye.*" He is speaking very clearly here to the fact that you need to always see yourself as the chief of sinners. Too often, when bringing reproof, Christians see themselves as the one with the speck and their brother as the one with the beam. But you are always to see yourself as the person with the beam. **The ego, at all times, is the beam.** It is the selfness that you are constantly trying to crucify. If you'll recognize that, you will have the proper humility to minister to your brother in need.

If you're going to help a brother get the speck out of his eye, what should you do? If you love him, you're going to speak the correct doctrine to him. Yet, doctrine is worthless if it doesn't generate Christlikeness. So you must also *require* a godly lifestyle of him. Whenever there is no obvious pursuit of God, embracing of the cross, or abiding in the Vine, then you are going to be an instrument of God to bring chastisement and rebuke to him. The motive of it is going to be love, and the end of it is going to be that we all might be partakers of God's holiness.

I'm talking about provoking unto love and good works with your life, not just your words. I'm talking about provoking one another by your testimony, where people will look and say, "I want to be like that, praise God!" How loudly is your life living?

"When you've done it to the least of these, My brethren, you've done it to Me" (Matthew 25:40). Would you be willing to take the time and make the effort for Jesus? His judgment is, "No, you wouldn't if you won't do it for the least of these. No, you wouldn't do it unto Me Whom you have not seen when you can't do it to your brother whom you have."

Take the beam out of your own eye. Make sure that you don't have personal ambition or an agenda. Make sure that, in these judgments, you're not sharing *your* perceptions, *your* conscience, *your* preferences, or *your* experience. What is the Lord saying to this person right now that will deliver them for the glory of God?

You must embrace this principle of "the chief of sinners" - that spirit of humility that will enable you to adorn the towel and become servant of all. Not as some type of feigned humility, but seeing the privilege and the high calling to be used to build the Body of Christ. It's doing what comes natural if you're abiding in the Vine. There's no effort in serving. There's no effort in a humble spirit to the man that's abiding in the Vine. The humble man never thinks about humility. It's just all the natural outflow of the person of Jesus Christ.

CHAPTER SEVENTEEN

Christ's Personal Cross

Now, what does it mean to deny self—the ego, the spirit man, the real you? You see, the problem a lot of people have had over the years is that they thought the cross had to do with punishing the body—that it's asceticism. One of the dangers we have is that when we begin to fast, and have a sobriety, and seek God, many times we begin to have confidence in our actions. We begin to think that God is going to be somehow moved by our denying of ourselves. **God is not moved by your cross; He was moved by Jesus' cross. And God does not love us because of the cross of Jesus; the cross of Jesus is because God loved us. And the personal cross is not to get God to love us; it's because we love God.** But I have to choose to empty myself. How does the Scripture say it concerning Jesus?—"I came not to do My will, but the will of He that sent me" (John 6:38).

We quote those things just like there's nothing to it. Stop and think! Did you know that Jesus had a personal cross? I'm not talking about Golgotha's cross. The universal cross was the cross that He bore for you and I—where He was the sinless sacrifice, where He was made to be sin. I want to talk to you about Jesus' personal cross for just a moment.

The personal cross of Jesus, we know, is eternity past, but it first evidenced itself in Bethlehem. Can you imagine putting aside your deity and clothing yourself with humanity? And He humbled Himself, Philippians says, <u>even</u> to the death of the cross. **But the humility was the personal cross—the choice to subordinate to the will of God, to die to preference, to die to personal ease and gain, to have a reputation and be willing to set it aside—the personal cross—the cross of identifying with God.**

He was born under a reproach, and all of His young life through adolescence and young adulthood, the majority of people thought He was an illegitimate child, born out of wedlock. He was raised in modesty as the carpenter's son. That's what He was known as—not the Son of God, not Your Majesty. He's the carpenter's son. As an infant, He was exiled to Egypt because of the fear of Herod and the pride of man. He was a man of sorrows, acquainted with grief and pain, and men thought it was because of His sin and iniquity, but He was wounded for our transgressions and bruised for our iniquities.

I think many of us lose sight of His humility in setting aside His divinity. When I say *setting it aside*, I'm talking about how Jesus did not draw on His divinity. He was fully living in our midst as a man. We can't comprehend it. You don't think for a moment that He heard those snickers as He walked down the road? As He got older, you think that it didn't affect His heart when His own brothers mocked Him? "You're who? Who are you trying to put yourself off as?" *And He became of no reputation.*

You see, the problem that most of us have is this: **It's not the reputation that we want to have before men; it's the reputation we want to have in our own eyes.** It's thinking of ourselves more highly than we ought to think. It's the assumption that we deserve or we're worthy or we're maybe a little better than other people. And Jesus is calling us to a place, here, of personal denial.

Now, how does He say it more clearly? In Philippians 2, in reference to Jesus, the Scripture says that He learned obedience by the things that He what?—suffered. **The suffering of your personal cross is for the purpose of bringing forth the fruit of absolute obedience. You have not embraced the cross if you're not living a life of obedience, total submission, to the will of God.** If you still have confidence in your own decisions, your own wisdom, your own methods, your own agenda, you need to die. If there are still natural treasures that influence your decisions that distract you from the work of God, from the humility of serving the body, of emptying ourselves for the good of others, then you need to go to the cross. I don't think any of us would presume to say we're living in perfect obedience, which then drives us to that place of seeking God for wisdom. "What is it that yet lacks? What is it that is offensive to you? What is it that I can more yield to bring You glory?"

CHAPTER EIGHTEEN

Do What You Are Told

"**G**et behind me, Satan." How piercing that must have been when this sword of the Word of God went into Peter's soul. *"For thou savorest not the things that be of God, but those that be of men."* Now following that statement, He says, and this is what we've been looking at, *"If any man will come after me, let him deny himself..."* (Matthew 16:24). How easy it was for Peter to represent his perspective! "You know, Jesus, that's not going to work for me." How quickly do you inject your perspective, when God has already revealed his will? Jesus said, "I must go to Jerusalem." And Peter immediately replies, "Not so!" God revealed his will to you when He said, *"Go ye into all the world, and preach the gospel"* (Mark 16:15). But what grand excuses you can come up with, "Hey, I've got things to do. I'm busy. You know, it's not my personality." God commands you in Hebrews 10:25, "Forsake not the assembling of yourselves together... and even more as the day is approaching." But you say, "Well, you know, I just don't believe you have to do that. This is legalism. I don't know why my pastor tries to put me under some of this restraint and legalism!" Now I use these things as things you can relate to. We can talk about a lot of other aspects, but these are things that you are probably very familiar with.

How quick you are to speak contrary to the revealed will of God and try to justify yourself? Quit trying to build your twenty-first century American excuses. God is calling you to come and be with Him and His people, but you are saying "I can't. I have a job. I have a busy schedule. You know, I have liberties." **Don't call preferring self over Jesus a liberty**. That's called rebellion; it's not called a liberty. That's called disobedience; it's not called a liberty. That's called idolatry; it's not called liberty. The liberty is not what we choose against the revealed will of God, the intended purposes of God. Liberties must still be directed by the voice of the Holy Spirit. There's not one part of your life that you are allowed to retain possession of. There's not a religious life, work life, playtime life, school life. So many people have this misconception of what liberty is and who we are as Christians. We are slaves! Does that statement cause you to do anything other than rejoice? "Bless God, I've got rights!" You don't have any rights - except to choose to die for Jesus. And if you fail to use your right properly, then you also have the right to choose to go to hell. And those are the only choices that are in our power to make.

So you must ask yourself the question, "Am I living a religion without the Cross? Is this just religion? Do I go to church? Am I a religious person, or am I a disciple of Jesus Christ? Am I a good moral, religious person? Or am I a slave, a bond-slave compelled toward holiness and fellowship with the King of kings?"

Where's Your Mark?

In Galatians 6:17, the Apostle Paul talked about bearing the mark of the cross in his own body. That didn't mean that Paul had scars on his hands and his feet. The marks of Paul's crucifixion were the beatings and the trials and the rejection and the persecutions where he was the offscouring of the earth.

In the Greek, that word "mark" means stigma. Do you have a stigma on yourself in today's society? What makes you stand out, and how do people view you as a disciple of Jesus Christ? How bright is your light in this crooked and perverse generation? The Scripture makes it clear that there is no fellowship between light and darkness.

We've been told that the only way to reach people with the gospel is to befriend them and not offend anybody. And I want to tell you something. It's not about befriending, and it's not about not being offensive. It's about genuine love. See, Jesus did not befriend the world. He didn't become one of them. He wasn't buddy-buddy. He loved them and died for them. He became sin with their sin, but He wasn't their friend. He walked in the Spirit, which gave Him genuine compassion and love; but in no way did He ever embrace or endorse their ways.

Does the world still see you as one of them? It's one thing to have the world dead to you, but are you dead to the world? Are you concerned with what they may think of you? Or can you truthfully say, "You know, I really only care what Jesus thinks about me. Nothing the world says or does influences me. I'm not one of them. I don't care what they think about me. I am not going to dance to their tune."

CHAPTER TWENTY

Worthy To Be Called Disciple

Luke 14:26, *"If any man come to me, and hate not..."* the meaning of "hate" there is to "love less." It's not a hatred based upon offense or vindictiveness. It is a devaluing in comparison to your love for God. *"...And hate not his father, and mother, and wife, and children, and brethren, and sisters, yea, and his own life also..."* Then you won't get as many blessings as the obedient Christian? No. What does the Bible say here? *"...he cannot be my disciple."*

Hmmm. That's different than what most Christians would say. Today, people would say, "Well, that's for really zealous Christians." What other kind is there? "Well, that's for Christians that are just on fire for God." What other kind is there? *"...I would thou wert cold or hot. So then because thou art lukewarm, and neither cold nor hot, I will spew thee out of my mouth"* (Revelation 3:15-16). "Well, Corinthians tells us that Paul recognized that there were carnal Christians in the church." Yes, there were, and Paul demanded that they change. Not a lifetime of carnality. And if your response to that is, "Well, how long do I get?" then your time is up! You're justifying your carnality and not wanting to repent and honor God.

Are you too busy to be a zealous Christian who is on fire for God because of work? Then get less busy! "Well, if I lose my job..." What?

You might have to change your lifestyle? Is Christianity about a lifestyle? What does God want for you? Does God want for you to have a flat-screen TV or for your kids to have the fastest computers and coolest cell phones? Or does He want to get us into heaven and to have us represent Him in Christlikeness while we're here?

Not A Partnership

Galatians 2:20 says, "*I am crucified with Christ: nevertheless I live; yet not I, but Christ liveth in me: and the life which I now live in the flesh I live by the faith of the Son of God, who loved me, and gave himself for me.*" It is no longer I that live. The "I" is the ego. The "I" is the self that has the greatest of all of God's gifts: free will, volition, and choice. And the life that "I" (the entity) now live, I live by the faith of the Son of God. The "I" ego, dies. The "I" entity exclusively becomes a vessel and a servant of the will of God.

This life that you and I are living is not a partnership. How much of the old man is still recognizable in your own life? You know who you are. How much is still there? How much dominates the choice to die daily indicates to us the propensities are never going to go away. We all know that in us, that is in our flesh, dwells no good thing. That "no good thing" is you, the ego, and it constantly wants to rise up. And that "rising up" is not overt rebellion, for most of us. It's not immorality. It's not a life of living in hedonistic expressions. Rather, many will begin to scramble to the Word of God to try and justify choices to leave a little bit of self alive.

The cross is the yielding of choice to the wisdom and will of God. It is death to self, death to ambition, and death to independence. There is nothing more frightening than truly releasing everything to God when you don't know your loving heavenly Father. He's going to do what's best for you. He is a good God. All that you can control is your next choice. Does your world seem like it's out of control, and you can't do anything with what's happening around you? You do have control of one thing: the next choice you make, the choice to resign yourself to the will of God, the choice to boast and to praise in the midst of adversities, the choice to serve others instead of yourselves, and the choice to really step back and ask, "What is it that's going to bring glory to God at this time in my life?"

Created For His Glory

There was a book recently published that, in essence, said that life is about man being happy in his service to God (so God got some billing in the book), and that man is to be happy and to enjoy and to delight in his service to God. I'd like to address it from a little different perspective: life is not about you being happy, it's about God being glorified.

Now, Father is not opposed to you enjoying life, and He is the author of every good and perfect gift, and He is the source of your joy. *Joy I give to you, not as the world gives,* praise God! So, then, what you have to do is step back and say, "What is the source of my happiness? What is the source of my joy?" And it can't be God living to make you happy. It has to be your life living to glorify Him. If God is glorified, I'm happy! If I'm miserable, oppressed and suffering yet God is glorified, I'm happy, praise God!

It's a process to get there, and we're all going through it. It would be great to arrive at that and have it remain; but the fact is it ebbs and flows, doesn't it? But until you get that basic premise down, you're always going to be out on the fringes in your thinking, where Satan can inject thoughts that bring confusion and doubt in your mind as to what the priority should be in your life. And I want to tell you something. Your

I Die Daily

job is not your priority. Your family is not your priority. Mankind is not your priority. We were created by Him and for Him.

How much of a pull is there out of the presence of God into the presence of man? Which satisfies you more? Which demands the most of your attention? How many of you are ready to sit and listen to all of the needs of your friends and your family and your loved ones or to be able to care for their needs? These things are good in and of themselves, but where are they on the priority list? What's the question that I'm asking? Which is most common to you? Which is the easiest to do: spend an hour with a friend or an hour with God? Which is second nature to you? Getting up and going to work, or getting up and having communion with God? If you had to make a choice, which would you choose? "Well, I have to go to work. If I don't, they'll fire me, and then I'll starve and die. We all know that the whole purpose for me being on this planet is to retire at forty and have life easy." How vexed are you in what is really the purpose of our being? That is the not the reason God created you. Is the way you are living in this current life the best it can be for the glory of God?

I'm talking about the appetite to be with God, because I want to tell you something, beloved, it's possible to pray without ceasing. It's possible to exist and live in constant communion with God no matter where you are or what you're doing and to be aware that the reason I am where I am at this moment, in this business meeting, on this call - whatever it might be - is to glorify God. Don't think for a moment that God's call and best for your life is you just making a living and getting through the day.

Do you look at this Word and go, "You know, I would like to do more, but my job. I would like to do more, but my schedule. I would like to spend more time with God, but..." You are distracted, and you are vexed.

The good news is Father is merciful and loving and kind and longsuffering. So maybe I'll get a second chance. The Lord is merciful. Maybe I will get a second chance. Possibly I will, then, be able to get into heaven. Maybe I will, then, be able to experience the blessings of the Lord. Maybe I…and isn't it tragic that even in that thinking, the emphasis is self instead of a heart that desires to be willingly obedient because He deserves it, praise God! Because He's holy, because He's majestic, because He's an awesome God.

CHAPTER TWENTY-THREE

God Can Use Dead Men

I've been going back and refreshing myself with some of the great prayers over history. How many of you have ever heard the name of David Brainerd? One of the great prayer warriors. You know, he reached very few people for Jesus. He died at thirty, and all he did was wander around the Northeast praying in the woods. Has anybody heard of a great American Indian revival? He was praying for the American Indians, the Susquehanna primarily and up in this area, and just praying days and hours and weeks on end! He had no interpreters. One of the first meetings he had as he was praying and interceding for the Native Indians of our land, was in the early 1700s. He was just on his face praying for God to bring a revival and to save American Indians. Every once in a while he'd run into a drunken Indian somewhere that would be his interpreter. Can you imagine what those messages must have been? Even then, though, there were some saved. But, you know, the life of David Brainerd wasn't just about the Susquehanna Indians. Other young men's hearts were smitten by a man who could go out supernaturally and cry out to God and be used by the Holy Ghost and reach a people that he couldn't even speak to; so then possibly God could use them in the miraculous.

There were a few men that were touched by this (like Hudson Taylor and the Wesleys) who all point back and talk about David Brainerd and a life that was poured out in intercession. He was a man that traveled lightly as it pertained to the recognition, the glory, the weights of this world, and the comforts of this world. As a seed that falls into the ground, he died, but he didn't remain alone. Lives were touched far beyond anything that could be imagined.

F.B. Meyer said that one day Hudson Taylor was in his house and said, "Jesus spoke to me today and said, *I'm going to reach Inland China, and if you would walk with Me, I could use you.*" Powerful statement! God said, "I am going to do this… and if you'll hang out with Me, I'll use you." Do you understand the Greater One that indwells you? Do understand the potential that's in you? Do you understand what could happen if your priorities changed? Begin to lighten up your load a little bit, and let the weightier things, the eternal things, begin to be the priority of your life? Begin to pray for souls and ask God, "If possible, use me in this generation, use me on this campus, use me on this job, use me in this neighborhood."

You see, the reason that you are not being used in that supernatural way is because you've not embraced the cross. You think you have, but there'll be fruit. There'll be evidence of a life that's been offered up and the continual process of this <u>willingness</u> to die.

CHAPTER TWENTY-FOUR

Resignation to God's Will

Let's talk about the cross of resignation. It is the cross that resigns itself to the will of the Lord. Your Father is loving, and He entertains your heart's cry. Do not ever be afraid to share your heart with your Father, as Jesus did in the Garden of Gethsemane. "I don't like this. I would rather have that. Here's what I see. With my limited knowledge, this is what makes sense to me. Nevertheless, not my will but Thy will be done. If it be possible, let this cup pass. If not, give me the grace to drink it, for there is nothing I want more than for You to be glorified in my life." And that glorification might be your death, the death of your spouse, the death of your children, the destruction of your reputation, or the diminishing of all of your resources. To the natural mind, those all sound like negative things. But how can they be negative if they are for God's glory? How can they be negative when they all work for good from the eternal perspective? Are you dead yet? That little list that I just ran through, does it cause trepidation in your heart? Does it cause some kind of panic in your life? Does it cause you to say, "But what if God wants 'this'?" Do you mean you haven't given it to Him yet? The thing that causes you to be afraid that God wants something from you is the very indicator that you still possess it. You're still holding on, even though you're saying, "I'm dying daily. Everything that I have is the Lord's."

Resignation to God's Will

Here is a little prayer I heard and wrote down in my Bible over the years: "Lord, I'm willing to receive what You give, to lack what You withhold, and to relinquish what You take." Some of us can't receive what God gives, because we have this false humility. What if, in the midst of economic oppression, God decides to just bless your socks off? Do you have the humility to be blessed, while everybody else is being oppressed, and see it as the will of God? God can tell you how to use it, or would you feel better about yourself if you gave up yours because everybody else doesn't have it? Did God tell you to? Do you have the faith? Do you have the humility? Are you subordinate enough to the will and the sovereignty of God to receive what He gives you? What about when He wants to give you adversity and trials? Not my will, Thy will be done.

God in His sovereignty gave you liberty and license to make choices. Do you understand that, as creatures in the image of God, choice, will, and volition are not subject to the sovereignty of God? I'm not saying that it will make a final determination on the plan and the will of God, because He will work your will for His glory. It doesn't matter what you will, what you do, or what you choose. God's going to be glorified! Don't misunderstand what I am saying. You have a precious gift in will, but are you using it properly by resigning it to God's control? And with that resignation comes the ability to rest in the goodness, the wisdom, and the grace of God. There is nothing that you have within yourself to change any of the circumstances that you are facing. Your next choice can only be to boast in God and believe for the grace to drink whatever cup He hands you, because God is good, and His ways are perfect.

CHAPTER TWENTY-FIVE

Will You Follow?

J esus once asked a man to follow Him, but the man said, "Let me first bury my father." And how did Jesus respond? "Let the dead bury the dead." People seem to think that's a harsh thing. This isn't saying that Dad was lying up on the slab, and Jesus said, "Let the dead bury the dead." In fact, if you study historically, they had to bury the dead within one day. What this man was asking was actually this, "My parents are old. I need to go back. Let me go back and set things in order and make sure that everything is well and that I can see my dad through his last days, and then when he passes and I'm sure that everything is comfortable and stable, I'll come." So Jesus said, "What have I done to you? Let the dead bury their dead." There's a new kingdom. There's a citizenship in the kingdom of God that makes you no longer an earth-dweller. Your commitment cannot be to your natural family, your culture, your ambitions, or your patriotism.

Fenelon said "Get rid of everything that hinders you from turning easily to God." When God speaks, how easily can you get with His program, or is there something hindering you? Do you have yourself bowed down, obligated, and in bondage? How loosely are you holding everything? How willing are you, if just like Matthew, the Lord says, "Come and follow Me," and you say, "Well, you know, wait a minute,

Jesus. I've got to go on a short sale." You want me to tell you how short a sale God expects? Walk away! Matthew did! Are you ready to do the will of God? You think, *"God would never have me walk out on my equity."* What if He did? *"Get behind me, Satan!"* Do you have any treasures? *"Well, you know, wisdom would say..."* Okay, but what is the voice of God saying right now? Look to the eternal wisdom of obedience to the Word of God, not natural wisdom.

If you came to me and said, "Pastor, I believe God told me to just walk off today and head to Africa and leave everything behind" then here's what my counsel would be. How about leaving it all before you leave it all? You can't live a life in bondage to material things, and then think you're ready to leave it all in a moment's notice. I would also encourage you to not think that is a noble statement. Let me tell you what is more noble, doing what God told you to do. It may be more noble for you to stay here, keep your job up, witness to people, and raise your family. That could be the most noble thing you could do rather than going to Africa. Because it's not about what you're doing; it's about whether you're doing it in obedience to God.

The Cross is Obedience

The cross is obedience. You might say, "This is so hard!"—but it is the same for all of us. There is nothing that is not common to man, and it wasn't easy for Jesus. In agony, He prayed more earnestly. He sweat drops of blood and agonized until He could cry out, "Not my will, Thy will be done." There is no easy road. The Son of God learned obedience by the things that He suffered (Hebrews 5:8), having humbled Himself. The cross is nothing less than obedience to the call of God, the will of God in your life

If you haven't embraced the obedience of our Lord to the cross then you are in danger of treading the blood of Jesus beneath your feet. There remains no other access to communion and fellowship with God. You are endangering yourself by setting your own standards, your own parameters of what God can have. I want to tell you something. You need to sit down and count the cost. What more tragic thing could possibly happen than being in that bondage of self-deception, of having lied to yourself and others lied to you, and walk up to that throne with absolute confidence, and hear, "Depart from Me"? And your rebuttal is, "Lord, I preached! I cast out devils!" And He will say, "I never knew you. I never approved of you. I never sat on the throne of your life. Yes, you cast out devils—to try to stay out of hell, not to love, worship, and

The Cross is Obedience

honor Me. Yes, you preached the gospel—as works." You were receiving your fulfillment and gratification, but it's not about you feeling good. It's not about you doing good things. It's about Jesus being Lord and Him being the reason that you live.

What is lacking besides your brokenness and your surrender and your choice to die? 2 Peter 1:3 says that God has given you all things that pertain to life and godliness. What more do you want? You have a great cloud of witnesses, whose faith you can follow. You have the presence of the Holy Spirit and the blood of Jesus Christ. And you are where in this journey after so many years? You just don't want to die. And it's not just because you're selfish. You are afraid to die because you don't know God. You absolutely don't believe that Father has your best interest. What an indictment against God! "If I give everything to God, He's just going to ruin my life." I want to tell you something. If you save your life, you will lose it. I would encourage you to get to know your Father. He is loving, merciful, and compassionate; and His intentions for you are good. He is the Father of lights, the giver of every good and perfect gift (James 1:17).

CHAPTER TWENTY-SEVEN

Love Him More

Why do you need to go to the cross? It's not to earn God's approval; He already loves you. You go to the cross to be able to love Him more. Don't you want to love Jesus more than you love Him right now? You can still love Him more, and the way you can love God more is to love yourself less. Every day that you wake up and take a breath is a battle of self-love. The fact is, in the natural, you love yourself first and foremost.

Jesus said that if you don't love Him more than yourself, you're not worthy of Him and cannot be His disciple. *"For which of you* [verse 28] *intending to build a tower, sitteth not down first, and counteth the cost, whether he have sufficient to finish it?"* Have you considered what it's going to cost to finish this course? Do you make bold declarations of, "I love you, Lord" when you should just say, "Lord, thou knowest"? That's how Peter replied on that day in Galilee when Jesus asked him, "Do you love me more than these?" Last time, Peter made bold declarations that he would die for the Lord; but this time, he just says, "You know."

How can you say, "Lord, I'm willing to die for you," if you're not willing to die to self in the small things? How can you die for Him if you can't live for Him? What makes you think you're going to stand up under the adversity that's coming if you are failing in the small choices?

Do you choose to miss church because of sickness, but then you get up the next morning and go to work just as sick as you were the night before? Does inclement weather keep you home, when you used to drive through piles of snow to get to church because you valued the opportunity to be with the saints in the house of the Lord? I'm just trying to point out the small things. How much of the cross do you still need to embrace? What is your treasure? What excites you? What are you living for? What are you giving your life for? Ambition? Pride? Lust? Worldliness?—and by that I just mean being an earth dweller. Are you caught up with the cares of this world?

How strong is that voice of self? How much does it dictate your life? Can you hear and comprehend the voice of self more clearly than the voice of God? Can you distinguish between the two? I believe in these last days that is the most critical task at hand. You must have the ability to learn the voice of God and distinguish it from the voice of self.

Beloved, if you find yourself falling short right now, and you're saying, "I know that I'm not doing everything that I can. I know that there are areas in my life that are not surrendered totally to God." Just repent. Come into the light, as 1 John says, and walk in the light as He is in the light. Put yourself in communion and fellowship with His Spirit and with those pursuers who by faith and patience are inheriting the promises of God. Don't have so much pride to think you have to do it on your own, and His blood will cleanse you from all unrighteousness.

CHAPTER TWENTY-EIGHT

The World is Crucified to Me

What are the treasures today that want to raise their heads in your life? Which are other than the Pearl of Great Price? Life is not about averting tragedy, trials, and adversities. It's about becoming Christlike. It's about the pure, spotless bride for which Jesus is coming. It's about the world being crucified to you, as it says in Galatians 6:14. Most of us emphasize *us* being crucified to the world, but the world must be crucified to *us*. What does "to be crucified" mean? It means "to be put to death and to be under." So the world, worldliness, and worldly wisdom must be dead to you. They must be put under the power of God's will. You are in the world, but you are not of it. You use it, but you don't abuse it.

The things of this world are lawful, but they are not all necessary or expedient. What has become necessary to you in this world? How about your job? Right now, how many of you believe that you are at the place where Matthew was? Can the Spirit of God speak to your heart right now and say, "I want you to quit your job; I have something for you to do."? Can you even hear that voice? Or would you deny that it's the voice of God? If so, your theology may be that "God is my source," but you actually trust in your job, not God

Is the world dead to you? How much of its wisdom do you still use? How many of its pleasures do you have to partake of to make you content? You've given too much credibility to the world by putting too much worth on it and not enough worth on the Pearl of Great Price.

CHAPTER TWENTY-NINE

Persecution

Our president just recently endorsed and promoted a nice, new Islamic stamp to be released just in time for Christmas. An act that is just blatant, and it's only the beginning of what we're going to experience in the opposition of the true gospel. There was also a public school recently that was mandating that the children learn to pray to Allah and requiring them to read from the Koran, in a time when the Bible is not allowed in schools, and the name of Jesus can't be spoken. In the news, I heard a story about parents that were told not to share their faith with their children, and the courts were mandating them to send their kids to public school so the kids could be more tolerant and have a broader world view.

We're at war! You could very likely lose your job because of the name of Jesus. There are some that are going to go to jail, and some that will even die in this generation in the near future because of the name of Jesus. If this sounds foreign to you, stop and remember that this last year around the world, there were a hundred and sixty thousand people martyred for the name of Jesus. It's just not in your neighborhood. But it's here. How are you going to respond to that? What are you doing to prepare yourself?

The best possible method of preparation is going to be the ability to take up that daily cross. In doing so, you will be preparing yourself for many difficult decisions. But the decisions you are going to have to make are only going to be tough when you're still alive and worrying about your reputation, what people think about you, and what it's going to cost you.

We are such a privileged and soft people. We think persecution is a strange thing that should not happen to us. Why would you sit there and ask, "Why is this happening?" when the Head of the church said it was going to happen?

Persecution is coming. That can seem to be a heavy message at times, and it might cause you to ask for something good to talk about instead. What's good is all that live godly in Christ Jesus shall suffer persecution (2 Timothy 3:12). Praise God! The good thing is you're living godly in Christ Jesus. Emphasize those positives and realize that the era is coming where the true gospel is not going to be tolerated in our society.

Weights, Sins, and Distractions

Hebrews 12 talks about the need to lay aside every weight and the sin and to run with patience the race that's set before you. Run with an established endurance. Run light. Get rid of the sins. Get rid of the weights that beset you, that hold you in their power. Is Father putting His finger on different areas of your life, and saying, "You know…you can travel a little bit lighter"? Lay aside the weights and the sin. Let's not mistake what's being said here. All unrighteousness is sin. Adultery and fornication are absolutely no more damning than self-righteousness and independence. Weights can be your philosophies, thought processes, possessions, or activities. You need to be in a place where there's nothing that holds you.

Does anything have a hold on you today? "All things are lawful, but all things are not necessary, and I'll not be under the power of any" (1 Corinthians 6:12). Is there a fear that has power over you? Are you afraid of losing all of your material possessions? Are you afraid of losing your image in the eyes of men? Are you afraid of losing your children? Does that have power over you? Does it affect the way that you bring the Word, the way that you live your life, the direction that you set for your household?

See, Jesus was absolutely free to do the will of Father. Nothing had

Weights, Sins, and Distractions

a hold on Him. Men didn't have a hold on Him. It said He didn't give Himself to men. He wasn't committed to men. He didn't depend upon them. He didn't care what they thought. He was here to do the will of the Father.

So, run with patience the race that's set before you and look to Jesus the author and the finisher of your faith. Consider Him, who endured the contradictions of sinners and was a reproach in the eyes of men. Then you will realize that He learned obedience through the things that he suffered. He learned that absolute obedience is what pleases God and brings the most glory to Him. It's amazing how you're willing to die and give up ninety-nine percent if you can hold that one percent. Do we ourselves define what death to self is? Or will we let God define what our death to self will be?

Distractions

What if you had the opportunity to move forward to the moment when you see God face to face? What do you think are going to be your treasures then? Will they be things that are vanity, vexation, cares of this world, distractions that have you in their grip? Do you think you'll care about what brand of clothes you wore, or what home you lived in, or whether the floor was scrubbed just right? Will you be wishing you watched just one more football game? Will any of that matter when you stand before the One who was crucified for you? Or do you think you'll be wishing you had taken that opportunity to share the gospel with a lost soul? Wishing you had spent more time in true prayer?

Are you putting yourself aside in that prayer chamber where it's quiet and staying there long enough? How do you know when it's long enough? When you leave and you're changed. That could be five minutes, or it could be five hours. Do you get up reluctantly, saying, "I can't wait to steal that next moment to be able to fellowship with God, to hear His voice, to see His Word, to speak from the housetops what I heard in the prayer chamber"? Has the zeal of His house eaten you up?

The question I'm asking is: Are you as diligent about the things of God as you are about the mundane? Because where your treasure is,

Distractions

there will your heart be also. These things, in and of themselves, are not evil or bad. But where is your heart? Where are your treasures? What excites you?

You know, my mind goes back to the passages about Jesus. You remember when He was a little boy and He was missing and they were looking all over for Him? He was perplexed that they didn't know where to find Him. When you're late coming home, does your wife know where to find you? I wonder what she's thinking? When your kids are late coming in is the question, "Oh I wonder, I hope they're not out partying," or is it, "Praise God, they must really be winning some souls tonight. I tell you what, God must be moving!" Do you know where to find them? In Father's house? "The zeal of Your house has eaten me up. I need to be about my Father's business," praise God!

Are your kids becoming earth dwellers, making their decisions based on vocational ambitions or family traditions? If so, they're not producing the fruit that's going to honor God. They need to be holy! They need to be separate unto God! There can be no trace of this world in them, the world's wisdom, the world's methods, the world's treasures. It is your job as a parent to say, "Wait a minute. What's being produced here?" Because one of two things is happening: They're either abiding in the Vine or they're abiding in the world. If there is any indication of abiding in the Vine, there will be fruit that God recognizes, and He will purge it so it will bring more fruit.

How many distractions are you now choosing to set aside? Are you traveling lighter than you were last week in this journey to the lordship of Jesus, the glory of God, and the death of self? Are you putting off the weights and the sins? Are you pulling off all of those tentacles of the world that have come in and engulfed you? Be free from those things, and let the robe of righteousness be very apparent again in your life.